T0142420

M. A. Benjamin

Illustrated by Wilma McDaniel and M. A. Benjamin

WHEN I PRAY
The Lord's Prayer

© 2009, 2020 M. A. Benjamin Illustrated by M.A. Benjamin and Wilma McDaniel. All rights reserved.

No part of this book may be reproduced, stored in a retrieval system, or
transmitted by any means without the written permission of the author.

AuthorHouse™
1663 Liberty Drive
Bloomington, IN 47403
www.authorhouse.com
Phone: 833-262-8899

Because of the dynamic nature of the Internet, any web addresses or links contained in this book may have changed
since publication and may no longer be valid. The views expressed in this work are solely those of the author and do not
necessarily reflect the views of the publisher, and the publisher hereby disclaims any responsibility for them.

This book is printed on acid-free paper.

ISBN: 978-1-4389-6317-4 (sc)
ISBN: 978-1-7283-7152-8 (e)

Print information available on the last page.

Published by AuthorHouse 11/24/2020

authorHOUSE®

This book is dedicated to our grandchildren

Desteny G, Faith H, Anna M, Hope H
Xavier F, Janae H, Elijah P, Xalya F
Xandria F, Xander T, Ezekiel M

by: Desteny G.

Our Father who art in heaven...
(Father GOD lives in heaven)

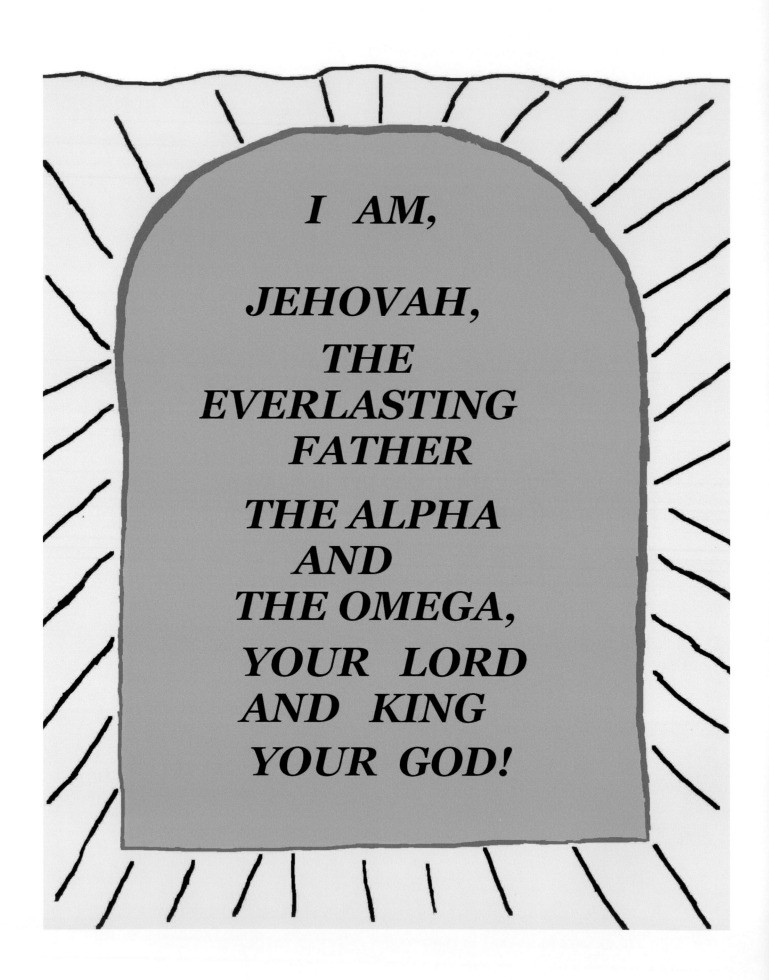

Hallowed be thy name...
(HIS name is holy)

Thy kingdom come, Thy will be done...
(GOD wants us to obey his rules, just
like we obey our parents rules.)

On earth as it is in heaven
(We can only ask for things HE would approve of)

Give us this day our daily bread,
(HE supplies everything for us)

Forgive us our debts, as we forgive our debtors
(we have to forgive others so HE will
forgive us our wrong doings)

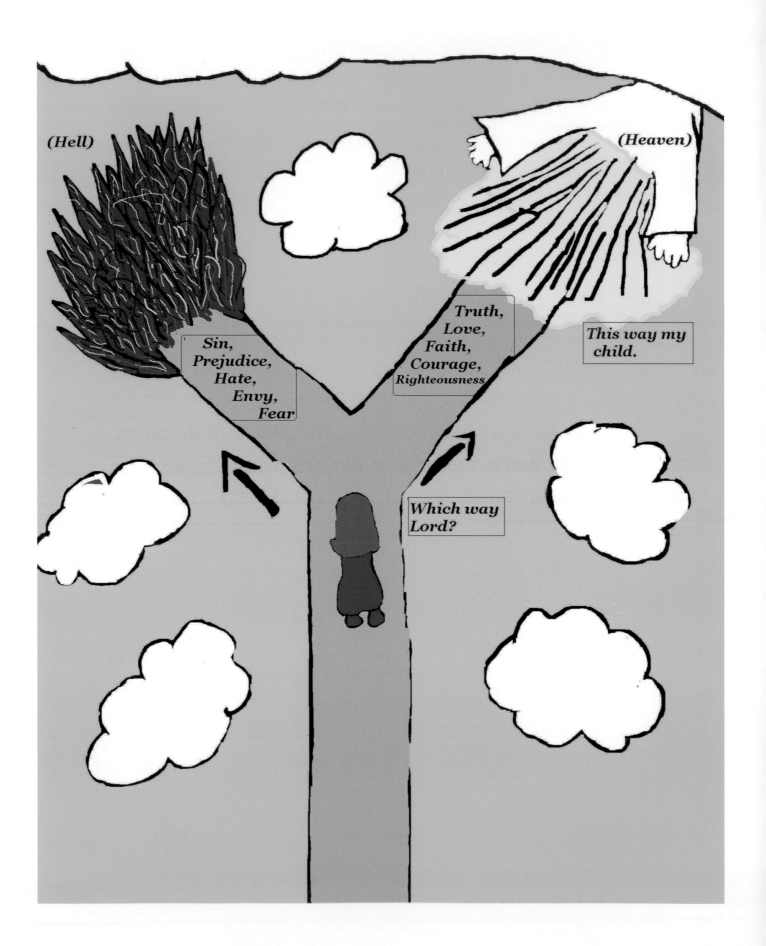

Lead us not into temptation, but deliver us from evil
(We have free will but if we ask HIM HE
will help us make the correct choices)

For thine is the kingdom

The power and the glory
(Father GOD has the power and we give HIM praise
whenever we worship HIM in songs and in our prayers)

Forever and ever...Amen.

Printed in the United States
By Bookmasters